Spirited Bliss

The Soulful Journey To The Different Spirit Realms

Suzanne Ebby (Word Weaver)

BookLeaf Publishing

India | USA | UK

Dedication

To all whose unsaid, unheard and unmet words for being too unruly, unusual, untamed and unchecked. To all rambling runaways trapped in emotional, physical and spiritual rampage.

Preface

The discipline or patience required for good story telling pursuits are beyond my reach. I guess I am good at putting words together like a puzzle or painting a picture in words, I love being a freestyle lyrical vocalist. My love for writing had to be conveyed to the world, so here I am enjoying every bit of articulating my turbulent emotions in poetry, with the only hope that I am causing toe-curling, heart fluttering, hormone fluctuating sensations for all my readers out there.

Disclaimer: This collection of poems is not for the faint-hearted, overly pious and religious fanatics, relatives and minors. I am a responsible adult!

Acknowledgements

Over the last one year, I have been a trying to find ways to transform my frustrations to a very productive state of mind. That's how I started writing poetry. While I always had a flair for musical eccentricities, the reason for me to put my thoughts into a frame and not forget to save it on my phone, is my sister. **Sarah (Nao)** *you are my biggest supporter, my greatest fan and my absolute nightmare critic. Chechi loves you, always.*

Amma and Appa, *I thank God for the creative and literary genes in me. However, guys, please don't read my poems. They are parental in-appropriate.*

I thank **God**, *giving all glory to Him, who has blessed me with the talent for writing, singing and reading.*
To all the moral policing people who may say that my poems are "explicit and vulgar", please let me remind you, I enjoy all genres of literature that includes romance, mental health, love, sacrifice and even a smidge of spice!

I want to acknowledge a certain English teacher Mr **Eskelin Gonzales**, *who was my teacher in class seven. Sir, I don't know if you will ever read my book, however, the* *reason I took up reading and writing is because of you, when you asked my dad to get me books to read instead of scolding me for getting one out of twenty in my dictation test. That catapulted my love for literature to soaring heights.*

My family away from my family. To **Betsy**, *my best friend, our bond stands the test of time. The last thirty years of friendship and sisterhood is all that needs be said to remind us everything in between. To* **Pooja chechi, Shereena, Alanto, Jomy and FebiEttan**, *you guys have been my rock and support. I know, you hate anything remotely close to reading and writing, but still, keep the copy of my book for my sake.*

Gayatri Padmanaban, *marvellous human being, resilient, gorgeous woman, I am proud of who you are, but above all for taking the time always to be there to listen to me rant, vent and destress no matter what.*

Shabistan, *thank you for giving me the shove and believing in my poems, that, it is worth publishing, when you posted my poem on Instagram, that was the first time, I felt that they were to be seen and heard.*

That brings me to **Vidit**. *Your take and interpretation on life, books and poetry has been always enlightening with* *a sprinkle of teasing. Grateful to you for being always kind to review my poems.*

*This eventually leads me to acknowledge my book club members **"Readers' Anonymous"**. Vibrant, colourful, writers and readers you guys are, and I am anxiously waiting for all your works to be revealed to the entire world.*

***Sara Abraham aka Bebuchechi**, thank you for encouraging me to apply to the Book Leaf publishing challenge, otherwise, I would have waited and waited till words collect dust.*

*Lastly, my crazy cousins **(Baidos) and Sharon chechi**, this book is for you, for screaming to the world that embracing topics such as feminity, sexuality, men (not boys) are part of who and what we are as women.*

*Finally, thank you the **Book Leaf Publishing House** for the twenty one day challenge and for prompting writers to showcase their words to the world. This Word Weaver is truly grateful to everyone.*

1. SENSUAL SPIRITS

Conquered Surrender

A gentle glow that warmed my heart with light.
She whispered secrets, sweet ministration in my ear,
While I made love to her, and felt the breeze near
Those crystal eyes and gazing blaze
No woman ever stood pretty in naked bliss
I touch her like heaven hosts
And I lose myself and all control.
No man or beast or God spoke
While we hashed out in nature's glow
There is a time to sing a song
This was what I cried , aloud howl
The universe is at breaking point
As we hurl, toss and scream together
The waves of seas, are all we hear
The sounds so sharp, it cuts like lightning
We fell in silence as we struggled to hold
Hurl, toss and scream together
We reached a peak and cried in softly
I whispered my love so roughly
While she smiles oh so brightly

A gentle glow that warmed my heart with light
He prayed dark secrets, desires unchecked
He made love to me, like no tomorrow
Darkened eyes, haunting gaze
Pulling me in a sea of praise
No man ever stood, in punishing ecstasy
His touch, caresses and burning fantasy
I lose myself of my steel resolve
As Sun, moon and stars dissolve
While I succumbed to his powerful role
Tears of joy, with continued brawl
I dipped, drowned, drank till my heart quenched
No lies, just harps and drum beats
We hurl, toss and scream together
I cry a shudder to remember forever
Drips of love, flowing like fiery ember
Stroke of midnight, time stands still
Hurl, toss and scream together
We reached a peak and cried in softly
He whispered, we've come to heaven's falls steadily
As I pray my prayers and smile brightly

2. The Star Crossed Lovers

The day begins with Sun's smile
The Sun knows me all too well
My skin's radiant and heat swells
The Sun beams proud, happy
The Sun's thoughts dwell
I will make you mine ,thoughts raunchy
I'll burn for you all day and night
No moon will be in sight
Oh my Sun , My sweet Sun
While you burn for me, I shiver for thee
The Sun strong rays , they blind
I close my eyes, the rays like rope
They cover my life and have me in binds
The Sun's love for me , never ends
For me, the Earth, my whole world, his.

3. What She Wants And What She Needs

His velvet voice deep like the ocean
Calm on the surface, strong in the motion
He staged a coup into many hearts
Capturing worlds from beyond the stars
Twisted, darkened eyes, strangling lies
He was the devil incarnate,
Manipulative, so dominate
Oh, he made women squirm, parched
Drinking in, thirsty, fully scorched
He plundered with heartless stares
He skinned women, none spared
What a woman wants, she doesn't know
But that's reserved for titles
Only red inked, in golden haunting bibles
Of romance, dark horse, wildest dreams
Don't be fooled by hues of Grey and Meadows
She fancies them ,in the page's shadow
What a woman needs, she surely knows
A green forest, spectacular Amazon
Be a hero, strong and powerful
Yet support her, soft, love bountiful
May she like her fiction, strong and brewing
but stay, her love for reality, bold and refining.

4. I Am Drunk For Her

She lay down, underneath me
I guide my hands on her deafening heart
My hands trail, navigating to worlds afar.
The desert flower in my hand I hold
She swells, her ravishing glow
I dip into the oasis of her.
My breath races, her breasts heave of hope
Her nipples blossom bright and bold
Waiting to be stroked and prod
I kiss and conquer till i find an expanse cave
The cave of squelch and dancing waves
I am a wretched man, intoxicated by her soul
My hand explores, for diamonds and gold
Her hand also touches my hard bold
I began to swell in her , hard with pride
We sway back and forth, till she is mine
Her tears stained eyes and wet refine
Delectable, beautiful, energetic and more
Her need for me , she presses hard
I come unravelling, in a sea of pearls
I have lost it, my sanity to her
I am a turbulent man, waiting to quarry her.
Again and again , we come undone
No fear to hold, no pain began

Till i hold her pants to my strong lips
Growl, roar aaaaaaaahhhhhhhhh, bliss
Yes, until I am left with only glad
I am an unquenchable, drunken bard
For all I need, her eyes to her overflowing valleys
Truly an exasperated man, I am left to be
Never again the same, left with new feelings.

5. The Mister

I first set my sights on you, oh mysterious mister
Away from the pack of drunken fools, you breathed cold
The night chilled its brazen teeth to awaken the alluring
heat
My eyes darted to feel the mist of your floated feet
As I approach you, hunger in me, start brimming desire
I reach out to intertwine, what's left of my insane
dignity
A bamboo reed, never can you, be indignantly broken
Your lips curl, to guide out your hissing snake
I hitch my breath away, at the dance of my luscious prey
Your eyes, they drown in my suffocating gasps
Your jagged lines, tempting me from the gates of
garments
I grab your hand and lead you to my guarded home
No names exchanged, only tarnished whispers and
glances
I pry away all that stands in between,
You are unhinged to any doubts, worries and scaring
fears
I sigh at my drudging initiations of unfurling you
I delve into your ravishing form of beauty and
perfection.
Not even king David can hold such mighty salutations.

Carved by the divine himself, giving life,
The sculpture is indeed an unruly temptation
You fondly cherish the touch of my wicked seductive
zephyr
You flinch and mutter curses so profound in aches
Starts to unsheathe under my enchantment and spells
Your mind, a calm sea of mystery,
become a torpedo of disarray, an unfurl of hidden deceit
Lies to not venture into the darkness that I hold
Lies to not desire the chaos that comes forth
I can sooth away all that's holding you at bay
Mister, I will have you one or the other way.

6. He Loves To Hate?

Once upon a time, beyond the Land of Shines
A young lass, weaving words and rhymes
Her strawberry stained hair, and striking flares
Strong headed and boisterous, so regale
Turning many men's heads, and green jealousy
Always unaware, oblivious and unruly
She stirred the heart of her arch enemy.
He loathed, sneered, was a rotten Mold
Waiting to strike, with chocking hold
But truth, stranger than fiction
Like pearls glitter in oysters, an apparition?
He dared an abominable dream,
hidden away, like unmatched thread in a tapestry
A vexation, to his inner demons
He longed to hold, what he couldn't summon
The object of his tribulation, his unparalleled desire.
He showed hatred to keep her at bay
But when night falls, he screams her name
Could she be his unravelling, or his utter ruin?
She chuckled, delighted at his secret
She toyed, pushed and pulled, to elicit
A equal opportunity for him to declare
His hatred, was all pretence.

7. The Maestro or the MasterChef?

He is like a master pianist
He stokes each key with a purpose
He knows every note, with his eyes closed
His long fingers float in dignified prose
His piano, is me and my body the keys
Pling, plank, plong the sounds marry
His fingers slowly circling my hilly glory
He pinches and probes with expert role
His digits tip toe to my gaping core
My very own, grip the sheets to curl and roll
He knocks on my flooded door
As he kneads me like a flour dough
Who is he? musician or chef magnanimous
But I arch harder to his greedy access
One, two and three, how many?
Are those talons that's ramming in me
A meal to be eaten, with hands only
Finger licking good or fine dining
His is a master with his hands
Knowing exactly where to land
All it takes is a touch, a twirl with those dafty hands
Does he lead his orchestra to grand stardom
Am I, his concerto, his opus magnum

Or am I, his breathtaking, saucy deliciosity,
All of these, have me, for his digits sought
Leads me to my scintillating thoughts,
Of his spirit filled, reviving, jazz phalanx
He, a Maestro or a chef, all learning, I climax.

8. GUARDED SPIRITS

Picture Perfect Frame

Splinter of woods, piercing worse than the others
Slow spills of chaos, like the maddening dark matter
Breaking and shattering, no longer picture perfect frame
To you the treacherous arrows of words, all just a game
I, perfect the pose, the praise of a laughable fool
Yet, my heart, my mind, wants to change the bloody rule
Of what's churning in me, to silence the sound
The voices that cry to break my very sane mound
Oh! I wish to beat down the blisters and blaze
Of pure agony, sorrow and depressing rage
How I wish, to scream, scram and hide away
From all of the submerging pressure, a lava awaits
To erupt the lament, dormant, insane volcano
All to subdue again and again, to mindless hollow.

9. The Treasure Hunters

The fog lifts to clear the ragged lines in between
To unravel the worlds of hypnotic worded tapestry
What mystery lies among the crude stones of lore?
Reveal the hidden temple, the deity of the silent songs
Oh! Alas! I see a fellow traveller, a strong willed lass
Quietly, she approaches, burning honey sea eyes
She is clothed with the pages from the book of
knowledge
Her hands, holding the papyrus of a wise lexicon sage
The weaves of letters, signalling like siren's
enchantments
Our etched path, archaeologists of the whispered
utterance
We hide from the spears of foolish discerning
We yearn for the treasures of profound concerning
The hollowed maze of unspoken interpretation
Leave us treading on the thin grounds of trepidation
To map and fortify the alluring magic of verbiage
We call fellow lettered scavengers and hunters to engage
The journey to unravel the temples of ethereal hush
Around the world, from holy grounds of gore to
romantic lush
To conquer the earths and skies of gilded breaths of
words.

10. Juvenile Guise

You ! Yes, you in the mirror
You, with the beast smearing terror
Waiting to prance and unleash
With growing fangs of guile preach
Your eyes deceive your respites inside
To devour the gullible rabbits in the field
No matter how hard it is to hide
The rush of your breaths are a brush of lies
For what you seek, the reflection of piety
Are to make you mirror an old stale deity.
The youth, fall to the sword of arrogance
The old, die to towers of penance.
What will your story be, with life in between
No matter, the option of your routines.
No man can completely hold control
To be a lighthouse to guide you to shore
So, my child, dig deep the tree of validation
Uproot the filth, the binds to the soil of self preservation
Let go, the yearn of the gauging immaturity
And be free from the juvenile guise of insecurity.

11. Dear Pen pal

Dear Pen pal
I write to you, with deep thoughts
I address you to my catapulting distraught
I sit, grasping to string words together
I wish, to let my tongue be soft like feather
For these sights of letters between us
Causes me to stutter like foolish mush
I fear that the sighs and songs I sing
Are too much or too little, my fear rings
Deeper into an abyss, a world drifting apart
Each parle strings, dissecting till sanity departs
You see, I don't know why I am a bumbling
Hoping my interactions would not come crumbling
While the buzzing creates a whirlpool of self doubt
Am I scaring you or pushing to be something I am not
I think twice, thrice and cross the speed of light
With my persistent paranoia, fearing my words bring
fright
I am not used to red letter days, or picture perfect ways
What will it take for you to remain my friend and stay?
What will it take for me not to panic and sway?
Yours sincerely, yet very truly,

A pen friend, uncertainly ?

12. Dr Strange - Madness of the Multiverse.

I am a mistress of the world of divided multiverse
Weaving thousands of scenarios, immensely diverse
Each time, spiralling into millions of chaotic suspense
My mind bends time, space, reality and blinding madness
What I see are visions of what if, what nots and whys
Why does my life alter, to criss-cross, and reasons defies
Jumping timelines, scenarios and infinite dystopian
fanaticism
Thoroughly defining the psych-shattering criticism
Will ever I cease the typhoon of surplus thoughts
Of overindulgence of self-doubts
Will I ever or will I not?

13. The Call

The grasp to give up, throw in the towel
Suffocating, gasping to the sweat of struggle
Silent screams to let someone hear
The call for the bold to be near

14. The Sentence

The silver, trickling from the author's blood
Turn black on the long parchment flood
The lives that are at the mercy of her pride
Makes me, yearn, to run away and hide
For her, I am, the heartless soul
Rising to stand as the valiant hero's foil
My heart stirs to burn the bridge
My hands wrangle to her despicable grip
Of her choke hold, as my sorted creator
her poisoned eyes, that of a puppeteer
They chant the lines that bind me to me
All I want is to be free, from blurry letters
For my arch, I am not a villainous quitter
Beyond the definition of my purposeful prison
My sword against her hand of disdainful pens
I plunge, through the worded spines
I will be whole, claiming only to be mine.

15. RAGING SPIRITS

Hello!

Hello! How may I help you?
This is, oh no, I am being bruised.
How dare, you run, hide from me!
Oh no, I'll run, till I am free,
Mam, are you okay, is this for real?
How may I help you? Please tell me dear.
He, is here, I am scared, darkening fears!
Oh no, you won't, stay right here.
Ah! You the devil, I am not your pyre,
Mam, please stay put, you are not anyone's lone desire.
I'll tie down, and take you to hell and back!
I'll fight you till my very breath lacks!
Quick to her rescue, we need to reach, before she sacks
No man will lay finger or torture on your beating heart.
No man will hold my aching heart!

16. The Traveller

The traveller once said "the road is not taken"
Is it straight or devastatingly flaked
The head screams, don't bend, go forth
The heart bellows, there may be not the true north
The compass, unsteady or broken?
Or am I, breaking free, not to be moulded
To the black and white, but never greys?
Can we live to lovely lies and stiffening truths
Or can we blur the lines or pretend to be couth
The nuances of life and death itself
Is the woo of illusion, the yearn for dilution
For love, gain and all bravado
Are lies in the eyes that sooth till tomorrow.

17. No Words, Lands, Only Spoils

Acid tongue, spears to lungs
Rancid stench, anger plunge
Walk the plank, drown the man!
Take the claim, strike the flame
Burn the bridges, hoist the colours
Run the world, hire the fowlers
No stone unturned, bloody Mary
So wars are hallowed, bullshit crazy
The children screamed, mothers wept
The baring dream, hells depth
wreath and smouldering ashes
defeat and pounding crashes
To hatred, fear and bellowing tears
All for a land to be called one's dear
Doesn't wring your heart
As even we all are a part
Never ending, pungent cycle
will it be catharsis, purely suicidal
can you stop this, enough period
or will it end with pain myriad?

18. Tie Me or Untie Me?

One day, each passing by
No matter how hard I try
I stay frightened to take a step
Into a world of unseen depth
For falling in love , a treacherous sea
Is it painful or a pleasure to be
Compassion, compromise and stealth
Am I made for this , or will I rebel
A woman, independent by caution
Always worried, riddled suspicion
Will a man truly love me
Will he chain me or set me free
Will binding rings be chocking strings
Marriage, an alluring hell,
Or, will it be a magic spell?
Illusion, reflections seen in mirrors
However, what I need is reality
With love, bound to eternity,
Yet, fly high, as fearless kites
While, all the eyes have sights.
Without regrets but only passion
Till the end of all deals and actions
With long love, yet full of freedom.
Never straining to avoid boredom

For this is not for the faintheart
For, we utter "till death do us apart"

19. SOULFUL SPIRITS

My Pain and Gain.

She looked ugly, weird and scrawny
She yelled and cried, nose runny
Yet when I held her, I knew instantly
I will never fully hate or love her completely
It's hard to think , a gift so dear
A pain in the rear like a bumper sticker,
The bane of my existence
Always striving for persistence
she is the only one, who is truly daringly enough
Brave enough to irk me, strong enough to save me
Always ready to fist me
But never once buff, realistically rough
All the while disowning me
for calling her ugly and gruff
Her analysis of life and death
Introspective, retrospective and critical
Jabbing me, always absurdly difficult.
We're like oil and water ,two different poles
Waiting to kick each other, fury groans
Battles so profound, filled with rages
For remotes, books, bread, stages

And boys and men of insane ages
Pillow fights, devoid of any prudence.
While having said this, there's evidence
For all our shared elements
Being recipients of death stares,
atrocious hand me downs and unpaid labourers,
Our common residence for 18 years
Force us to stay together, sly endears.
Unfathomable! I miss her crazy eyes
Those unchecked, scary dares
Her crude words like a perfect rain,
In the midst of our passionate jeers,
Are warmth during dark Decembers.
Like Bart and Lisa, Rachel and Leah
Our love for each other like turbulent weather
Strongly to say, Oh bother!
And it simmers down with a couple of beers
That while pulled apart, it's all quiet tears.

20. Are Trees Giant Leaves ?

Are trees giant leaves?
Do drops of water make the sea?
Do clouds bunch together
To make painting of skilful artistry?
Am I supposed to be, a masterpiece !
What grandeur splendour should I manifest?
Is it easy to keep up, with ever changing pace
No, never! It's harder to grow over a single day
Slow and yet steadily, I build myself up
To grow as tall as the trees, deep as the seas and as high
as clouds.

21. GRIM SPIRITS

Scarlet Red and the Wolf

I stared outside my window
Peaked to look behind the veil of shadows
The forest that held the secrets
For the call of the wild, intimidation rivets
They say beware, howl of a dark wolf
To be devoured , just by his looks
I agonise to see ahead of the woods
I, Scarlet Red, to run beyond the hood
For fear is my weapon, I feel lust siphon
to the eerie silence, my bead heightens
With wet folds, gnashing starlets
My precipice of haunting rivulets
I reach a house spun, Grandma's old rooms?
Those eyes beckon me, sinister looms?
Instincts, dread, a quivering arrow
Trepidations, I covet. I, a lewd sparrow
I know those eyes, hungry to devour
Oh! What big emerald gaze, a sight to hold?
That's to peak into your valleys and moulds
Oh! What long claws, they dig into one's skin ?
That's to caress, fondle what lies beyond the ruby lining

Oh! What razor sharp teeth, will they sink and draw
blood ?
Profoundly, I plan to devour and unleash a flood
My tongue will savour the dripping snatch
For I am the big bad wolf, what a catch.
For Scarlet, I will ravage you, till nothing is left.
My soul leaps, my core at unrest
My rose bud, pound, macabre lore
The big wolf is satiating, I yearn for more
I trail my reach, oh ! gobsmacked indeed
Oh what big ! I slither to the trembling heed
Oh what a big trunk ! will you give it to me?
It is a sacred tree, fruits hidden to be.
I, the wolf will give indeed,please promise to stay
To remain my unbridled, brittle, bold lay?
I am Scarlet, the wolf sees red, it's finally free to be
The despicable wolf or my unnerving self?
For you are the wolf, I hunt your animal whelve
For I shroud not in gardens of fear to stall
I am no longer, Little Red after all!

22. The Gaze Beyond The Mirror

Mirror! Mirror ! On the wall
Who is the fairest of them all?
Her voice, louder than drums of the world
Her eyes, are darts set on fire,
Barging into my soul's desire.
Her skin, the sands of time, can't shrivel away,
But Her blood streaked lips, never stutters
to spew the chants that makes Her deter
It's Her luscious golden poison apple.
Like the snake to the first man and his love
She is the dark plunge to perfect Snow
All this I gaze beyond my sight.
She, a witch to the hearts of many
She is my gift, I know it's blasphemy,
Unable to touch Her, my perverted delirium,
For Her end, is doomed by a certain flower.
But I will cherish Her, from the land of the far.
Who am I, you ask, let me reveal
I am, he who writes this doomed tale,
For my love, my cactus, my regale
I am he, who knows and sees all !
Only to be bound by facade and confines,
By the restraints of only false reflections.

23. Sleeping to Death's Beauty

Cursed to sleep for infinity, death is my name
While waiting to be revived by your soul's game
Will your blessed lips, awaken me
From the curse to be eternally unfree
My only error, to be of this world
Ruled by Maleficent, terror unfurled
Because of arrogance, to break the yearning spindle
The wretched division of man, magic, set to kindle
To set ablaze the fire of the strangled heart
Can love transcend beyond the realms of the depart ?
The dreams that keep me bound to the uncharted plane
Must be lifted by true love's kiss alone?
Or am I the only one, who can start breaking
From the chokes of grim reaper's harrowing.

24. Hooked !

I need to breath, gnashing fear
Gasping and gripping to stay clear
I take one look at this scarred, doomed soul
Have my mind, yielded to the villain's gore
He is a beast, a monster, vile and cynical
Trapping me with jest and prejudice debacle
Latching every word, while I am trapped as conquest
Mirroring every despicable, unwavering detest.
Oh! This infuriating burn that grips my wings
The fairy in me, Hooked by mesmerizing grins
Toying with me, kidnapped to lure uncertainty
While I, Tinker, with my thoughts of crude curiosity
Realising that I'll cherish his haze, so maniacal !
As he burns Neverland for my whimsical.

25. ROMANTIC SPIRITS

Lost Love

The church bells rang loud and clear
My heart banged too with all fears
As I saw him, I was brought to tears
He looks from far, straight right at me
Like arrows, my heart ripped and pierced
I sought for some clarity
He sought for some familiarity
A distant memory of his smile
Like a crumbled paper, waiting to rewrite
I was hurt, battered and bruised
Like a thorn to it's rose
A blessing or a curse
I turn to stop my heart bursts
He looks with a sigh
And finally waves old sweet goodbyes.

26. Love's Absurdity

Falling for you, was something, I never intended to do
Your quirks, perks and infinite wholesome world
Making my heart, pulse and beat, like butterfly flutter
Can I ever go back to a state of defiant pretence and
mutters?
Not knowing, how to cease my ramble or my addiction
My worship to your words, thoughts and vocal
edification
I may have fallen, further into a rabbit hole
Is too late for me, to forget and forgo
This new empire of deafening vulnerability
To what many may call, falling into love's absurdity.

27. The Queen and Her King

Pieces placed together, black and white
Lives being ordered to one king's right
The swift or the strong, not the one to fight
Beauty and brains are the keeping the strings tight
I will choose to use, fight and kill
All those in my way of adoration and spoils
My king, who are thou, for you my love
My foot soldiers, horsemen and all marvel
I'll get in their headspace to protect my own
I don't care, sacrifice and collateral
All for my man, to protect the battle.
None will be spared, I, the queen rule
Over devotion, life and death to wither
All is fair in love and war, come hither
Blinded they say, but truth be told
I have never been truly a sight to behold
Than where I stand, for you my solid rock
My heaven, my kingdom, my Lord
Check mate!

28. FREE SPIRITS

The Quiet Noice

The babbling brooks, coursing it's veins
Through the rough edges of the rocks pains
Intertwined with hands of the rows of blades
Searing from the clear blue sky
The mountains hold majestic bright cry
Laced with arousal of the misty sighs of the clouds
Lush forest blend to the rivers unfolding
Will the earth be a wonder lusting to be seen
With so much beauty, beyond the depths of fathom
Stillness and yet ever so restless
The nature bleeds to soak my soul
As in the quiet pounding i am made whole

29. The Melody Of Nature

I sit still, as the wind caresses my cheeks
His whispers, beyond the fathom of the meek
The grass, tickles my soft blushing skin
Their touch as reverence to a holy lint
The flowers sashay to the tune of the flute
The hymn from the lips of the bees, a salute
My heart brims to the melody of the wild
Singing to the rainbow as a naive little child
The stream skilfully spindles the earthly treasures
The water sprites beckoning me to heavenly leisure
The trickle of tears of the blue clouds , gracefully
enchants
among cosmos pastures, my soul dances and feet
prances.
The forest fairies sublime giggles, such a delight
The day bows to welcome the mighty star's bright
The night trumpets to the beauty of the silver gaze
I am charmed to surrender to the paths of abstracted
pace
To soon become one with blissful peace, mesmerizing
magic
Among the bees, the birds, the breeze, an absolute
romantic.

30. The End

A beautiful mind, a kaleidoscope of sights
All fragile and poignant, but one shatter, away from
lights